P9-DBS-655

LET'S
see

Farm Animals

by Jennifer Blizin Gillis

Content Adviser: Susan Thompson, Agriculture Communications,
College of Agriculture, Iowa State University

Reading Adviser: Rosemary Palmer, Ph.D.,
Department of Literacy, College of Education,
Boise State University

Let's See Library
Compass Point Books
Minneapolis, Minnesota

Special thanks to Lynn Mann, Manco Dairy Inc., Pittsboro, N.C., and the Cohn family of Matzah Rising Farm, Snow Camp, N.C.

Compass Point Books
3109 West 50th Street, #115
Minneapolis, MN 55410

Visit Compass Point Books on the Internet at *www.compasspointbooks.com*
or e-mail your request to *custserv@compasspointbooks.com*

On the cover: Dairy cows and a calf

Photographs ©: Joe McDonald/Corbis, cover; Corbis, 4; Bruce Coleman Inc./Ernest A. Janes, 6; Photo Network/Jeff Greenberg, 8; U.S. Department of Agriculture, 10, 14; Dwight Kuhn, 12; Unicorn Stock Photos/B.W. Hoffmann, 16; Photodisc, 18; Photo Network/Eric R. Berndt, 20.

Creative Director: Terri Foley
Managing Editor: Catherine Neitge
Editors: Brenda Haugen and Christianne Jones
Photo Researcher: Marcie C. Spence
Designers: Melissa Kes and Jaime Martens
Educational Consultant: Diane Smolinski

Library of Congress Cataloging-in-Publication Data
Gillis, Jennifer Blizin, 1950-
 Farm animals / by Jennifer B. Gillis.
   p. cm. — (Let's see library)
Includes bibliographical references (p.   ).
ISBN 0-7565-0670-0 (hardcover)
 1. Domestic animals—Juvenile literature. I. Title. II. Series.
 SF75.5G55 2003
 636—dc22   2003028293

Table of Contents

NOTE: In this book, words that are defined in the glossary
are in **bold** the first time they appear in the text.

Why Do Farmers Raise Animals?

Farmers raise **dairy** goats and dairy cows for their milk. They raise laying hens for their eggs. Most of the eggs we eat and the milk we drink come from animals on very large farms.

Farmers also raise animals as food for people to eat. Most of the meat we eat comes from large farms that have many animals. Farmers may raise beef cattle that are made into hamburger and steaks. Others may raise pigs that are made into bacon or pork chops.

Sometimes farmers raise animals to show at fairs.

◄ *Dairy cattle on a farm*

Dairy Goats

Dairy goats are raised by farmers for their milk. Some people with **allergies** drink goat's milk because it is easy to **digest.** Many people eat cheese made from goat's milk. Soap can even be made from goat's milk.

Only female goats give milk. They start giving milk when they are about a year old. Farmers milk goats two times each day. The goats eat **grain** from a **trough** while they are being milked.

Dairy Cows

Farmers raise dairy cows for their milk. Some dairy farms have hundreds of cows. Farmers milk dairy cows two or three times each day.

Dairy cows are born on a farm. They start giving milk when they are about 2 years old.

Dairy cows eat a lot. A cow can eat 90 pounds (41 kilograms) of food in one day. A hamburger a person might eat doesn't even weigh 1 pound!

Cows eat grass in the **pasture.** Farmers also feed them a mixture of corn, soybeans, oats, and other grains.

◄ *Dairy cows on a farm in Pennsylvania*

Beef Cattle

Farmers raise beef cattle for their meat. Hamburger, steaks, and roasts come from beef cattle.

Female cattle are called cows. Males are called bulls. Cows may have babies, called calves, once each year. Babies are usually born in pastures in the spring. They drink milk from their mothers' **udders** through the summer. In the fall, farmers move calves into **feedlots.** In feedlots, the calves are fed grain so they gain weight faster. The faster the calves gain weight, the faster they can be sold.

There are many different kinds of beef cattle. Black ones are called Angus. Cattle with red bodies and white faces are called Herefords.

◄ *Hereford cows and calves in a pasture*

Laying Hens

Laying hens are chickens raised for their eggs. Only hens, or female chickens, lay eggs.

On large farms, laying hens live in cages inside large buildings. They lay eggs that roll onto a **conveyor belt.** The belt moves the eggs into another room. There, machines wash the eggs, sort them by size, and pack them.

On smaller farms, hens may run around outside. They lay their eggs in boxes inside small henhouses. Farmers gather their eggs by hand.

◄ *A hen sits on a nest.*

Turkeys

Turkeys are large farm birds. Broad-breasted turkeys with white feathers are the kind most people eat.

Some farmers raise thousands of these turkeys at a time. On these farms, turkeys live in large buildings. On smaller farms, turkeys may stay in a pen outside during the day. At night, they go into a barn or building.

Baby turkeys that have just hatched from eggs are called poults. Turkeys that people eat are between 9 and 28 weeks old.

◄ *A flock of turkeys may include thousands of birds.*

Pigs

Farmers raise pigs for their meat. Bacon, pork chops, and ham come from pigs.

Most pigs are born on a farm. At first, baby pigs, called piglets, get milk from their mother. After a few weeks, they are eating a mixture of corn and other grains.

Pigs grow quickly. Piglets only weigh about 2½ pounds (1 kilogram), or about as much as a small bag of sugar. Fully grown pigs weigh more than 200 pounds (90 kilograms). That's about what a baby elephant weighs!

On farms, pigs live in special buildings or barns. Some pigs spend part of the time outside in pens.

◄ *Pigs on a farm in Wisconsin*

Sheep

Farmers raise sheep for their **wool** and for their meat.

Farmers shave off the sheep's wool each spring to keep them cool during the summer. This is called shearing.

Farmers may keep female sheep, called ewes, to **breed** so they will have baby lambs in the spring. Through the summer, the lambs drink milk from their mothers' udders and eat grass in the pasture.

Sheep that farmers raise for meat often are placed in feedlots in the fall. There, they are fed grain so they quickly gain weight. The quicker the sheep gain weight, the quicker they can be sold for meat.

◄ *Lambs stay close to the other sheep. One lamb drinks its mother's milk.*

What Are Some Animals That Help Farmers?

On large farms or ranches, farmers may ride horses to move groups of cows or sheep. They train some dogs to herd cows and sheep, too. The dogs bark and nip at the animals' heels to keep them with the rest of the group. Other dogs stay in the fields with farm animals and keep them safe from **predators.**

On many farms, cats live in barns and other buildings. They catch mice, rats, and snakes that come to eat leftover grain. Some geese make good helpers, too. They walk around the farm and chase or hiss at strangers to scare them away.

◄ *A ranch dog tries to get a calf back with the rest of the herd.*

Glossary

allergies—a body's sensitivity to things such as stings or food that cause sneezing, swelling, coughing, or sickness

breed—to bring two animals together so that they make babies; also, a kind of animal

conveyor belt—a machine with a large cloth or rubber belt that moves over rollers and can take things from one place to another

dairy—relating to milk cows and goats and milk products

digest—to break down food in the stomach

feedlots—large pens where many animals are kept and fed so that they will gain weight quickly

grain—seeds from plants such as corn, wheat, oats, and barley

pasture—a large field where animals can eat grass

predators—animals that hunt for other animals and eat them

trough—a long, low container used for feeding animals

udders—the baglike parts under cows' bellies where milk is made

wool—the hair of a sheep

Did You Know?

• On small farms, chicken or turkey houses may be on wheels. When the birds have eaten all the grass in one area, farmers can roll their houses to a new space.

• People drank goat's milk long before they began raising cows for their milk. Goats can live on land that is too dry for cows.

• Have you ever seen a fuzzy angora or mohair sweater? The wool comes from a goat that has very curly hair.

• Dogs that have the word *shepherd* in their name were raised to help herd cows, goats, or sheep. A German shepherd is a type of herding dog.

Want to Know More?

In the Library

Bell, Rachael. *Turkeys.* Chicago:
    Heinemann Library, 2000.

Murphy, Andy. *Out and About at the
    Dairy Farm.* Minneapolis: Picture
    Window Books, 2003.

Wolfman, Judy. *Life on a Chicken Farm.*
    Minneapolis: Carolrhoda Books Inc.,
    2002.

On the Web

For more information on *farm animals,*
use FactHound to track down Web sites
related to this book.

1. Go to *www.facthound.com*
2. Type in a search word related to this
    book or this book ID: 0756506700.
3. Click on the *Fetch It* button.

Your trusty FactHound will fetch the best
Web sites for you!

On the Road

Ardenwood Historic Farm
34600 Ardenwood Blvd.
Fremont, CA 94553
510/562-7275
To see how farming has changed
through the years

Kidwell Farm
2709 W. Ox Road
Herndon, VA 20171
703/437-9101
To see farm animals and go
on a hayride

Index

About the Author

Jennifer Blizin Gillis writes poetry and nonfiction books for children. She lives on a former dairy farm in Pittsboro, North Carolina, with her husband, a dog, and a cat. She is more of a gardener than a farmer, but has lived on farms and in farming communities.